THE NO NONSENSE LIBRARY

OTHER NO NONSENSE GUIDES:

Car Guides
Career Guides
Cooking Guides
Financial Guides
Health Guides
Legal Guides
Parenting Guides
Photography Guides
Real Estate Guides
Study Guides
Success Guides
Wine Guides

CARING FOR YOUR CAT

Elza Dinwiddie-Boyd

Longmeadow Press

CARING FOR YOUR CAT

Copyright © 1991 by Longmeadow Press

No Nonsense Career Guide is a trademark controlled by Longmeadow Press.

Published by Longmeadow Press, 201 High Ridge Road, Stamford, Connecticut 06904. No part of this book may be reproduced or used in any form or by any means, electronic or mechanical, including photocopying, recording, or by an information storage and retrieval system, without permission in writing from the publisher.

ISBN 0-681-41043-0

Production services: Marie Brown Associates
Cover and inside design: Ken Brown
Editing/copyediting: Karen Taylor
Typography: ANY Phototype, Inc.

Printed in the United States of America

0   9   8   7   6   5   4   3   2   1

CONTENTS

CONTENTS

ACKNOWLEDGMENTS

First let me thank <u>God</u> for creating cats and for giving me the strength to write about them. Then let me thank all of the cats who have shared my life over the years.

All books are team efforts and this one is no exception. A number of skilled people have worked together to make this book a reality. <u>Marie Brown</u> deserves very special recognition for coordinating and managing the effort. I am also especially indebted to her for her continuing support of my efforts to write. A special thank you to <u>Kenneth Brown</u> for designing the book and to <u>Karen D. Taylor</u> for a superb editing job.

A special thank you to <u>Adrienne Ingrum</u> for another opportunity and continuing support.

<u>Herb Boyd's</u> contribution to this manuscript is invaluable. His skilled writer/editor/teacher's eye knew just how to put a word here, or turn a phrase there. The superlative care he provides to our cats also deserves special recognition. And finally, thank you, <u>Ezra</u>, <u>Taft</u>, and <u>Simba</u> for so much love.

DEDICATION TO:

DAMU

He sits like a

sphinx

His ears alert with an

ancient instinct

To time the movement

of a passing prey

And spring like a Lynx

Herb Boyd

INTRODUCTION

Cats are wonderful pets. As myth and mysticism were replaced with reason and enlightenment, we came to better understand our little feline friends and to appreciate their supple beauty, grace, and fabulous company.

In recent years, the popularity of cats as pets has soared. Today, cats are but a few percentage points behind the All-American favorite pet, the dog. Cats as house pets are so common that the hackneyed phrase, "fighting like cats and dogs," has lost its accuracy because many cats and dogs currently coexist, peacefully sharing the same owner.

With its origin in Africa, the cat was the last of the animals to come in from the wilderness and become domesticated. In ancient Egypt, this mysterious newcomer, this voracious mouse killer and guardian of corn silos, was deified; to kill one accidentally could bring the penalty of death. These denizens of the courts of pharaohs, were secreted out of Egypt by Greek merchants who revered their superb mouse-hunting skills.

From Greece, domestic cats were dispersed around the world. These majestic and magical creatures became the Roman symbol of liberty and were venerated as gods in Buddhist temples. Despite a period of dreadful persecution during the Middle Ages, by the 18th century, French poet Gartier was referring to cats as "tigers that people can stroke."

Fiercely independent, aloof, capable of profoundly loving attachments to people, other cats and dogs, cats are never really tamed. The inscrutable pussycat is actually a creature of the wild who has deigned to live with humans for comfort and convenience. Enticed by the abundant food supply of mice in the Egyptian granaries, wild cats quickly adjusted to living among human beings. And until today, unlike the submissive dog or horse, a cat obeys its own needs and desires, keeps to its own schedule. A cat is trained, you might say, when the result of that training is to the cat's advantage.

To live with a cat, to be owned by a cat, to love a cat passionately, is to know that a cat's innate independence is also adorned by several irresistible attributes. They are gorgeous, stately, dignified, intelligent, fascinating, stimulating, humorous, and scrupulously clean. It is delightful to hold a cat and stroke its soft, warm, responsive, and furry body.

If you are the proud new owner of a cat or kitten, or if you are about to invite one to share your life, you have made a wonderful decision. Sharing one's life with a cat is a deeply rewarding and special experience.

CHAPTER ONE

Cats Are A Lasting Commitment

There is nothing that offers continuing fulfillment and satisfaction that does not entail great responsibility. That is what this book is all about: your responsibility to your cat. The first requirement of any pet owner is to be informed.

Responsibility

No matter how hopelessly in love you may be with a cute little kitten, you should carefully consider all the consequences of bringing it into your life. Many people who are enthralled by the cute antics of a kitten are not prepared to deal with the adolescent, adult, and old-age phases of the cat's development. The adolescent stage can be awkward and unattractive. When compared to the kitten, the prominent personality traits of the adult cat vary considerably. It is important to realize, when you make a commitment to a kitten, that you are making a commitment to a cat. Ask yourself these questions before bringing a feline into your home:

Will I be able to handle the daily chores that accompany the cat's presence in my home?

Will I be able to handle behavioral changes that will accompany various stages of the cat's growth and maturity?

Will I find the awkward, clumsy adolescent or adult as attractive as I find the kitten?

Will I be unnerved by the havoc the playful adolescent may create in my home?

How will I cope with the cat's shedding?

How will I react to the periods of aloofness that adult cats sometimes exhibit?

What will I do if the friskiness of the kitten appears in the adult as nervous, high-strung characteristics?

Am I prepared to nurse a sick cat back to health by cleaning wounds, force feeding, or administering medication to a difficult patient?

Am I prepared to make the cat's needs a permanent budget item?

Am I committed to the cat for the duration of its life? Far too many pets are rejected once they pass babyhood. Most of these rejects end up living miserable, short lives in streets, shelters, or animal experimentation centers.

Are you prepared to persevere, assist, and enjoy your cat's rites of passage and the changes in character, actions, and personality that come with maturing?

The life span of a cat ranges between 10 and 14 years. However, many well-cared for cats have lived to be 20 years old. So, you will want to consider the financial picture. Your cat will have continuing needs. You will need to allot a certain portion of the household budget to pay for the cat's care. It is important to plan ahead if you are operating on a tight budget. You do not want a shortage of cash to prevent your cat from getting the medical care it needs. Stash a tiny sum each week to cover unexpected or emergency visits to the veterinarian. Remember to include yearly check-ups in your budget.

Family Matters
Owning a cat is a family affair, so a certain level of commitment is required of each family member. At the very least, everyone in the household should express basic respect and a gentle attitude toward the cat. It is not a wise idea to bring one into an environment where there is an individual who dislikes them intensely.

Cats As Gifts
Sometimes people think it is cute to give a kitten to a child. Many kittens given to children wind up neglected or abandoned. Never give a kitten as a gift unless you are absolutely convinced that the owners are committed to a lifetime of care. Consult the adult who will have primary care responsibilities before deciding to give their child a living creature, unless you will supervise its care.

The Cruel Act Of Abandonment And How To Avoid it
If you take a cat in and find that you must get rid of it, do not abandon it—this is the epitome of irresponsible behavior. Dispel the erroneous idea that since cats are creatures of the wild, they can take care of themselves. The earth's environment has changed dramatically since domestic cats lived in the wild thousands of years ago. House pets exposed to the outdoors are subject to dying a miserable death.

Millions of abandoned cats suffer in the streets or in experimentation laboratories. Shelters that do not practice euthanasia on healthy animals are a viable alternative to abandonment. Be careful though, many shelters will take your cat in, and within a few hours, a vivacious, gorgeous animal will be killed.

There are many shelters that keep the animals until they are adopted. These shelters usually require a small fee. Many will only take healthy cats. You can also ask your vet, friends, relatives, and neighbors if they know of a good home for the cat you no longer wish to keep.

CHAPTER TWO

Choosing A Cat

Due to the severe problem of cat overpopulation, there are many cats available for adoption including pedigreed animals. Visit the various shelters in your area and ask to see the cats up for aodption. If you have your mind set on a particular breed, tell them exactly what you are looking for. If the cat you want is not available, ask the shelter to call you when a cat meeting your specifications is available. You can also call veterinarians. They usually know of cats who need homes. Tell all the cat lovers you know about the breed you want. Talk to groomers who specialize in cats. You will learn a lot about cats in the process and eventually find just the right pet. Remember, as you make the decision about how you will acquire your cat, overpopulation, heartless abandonment, and the resulting horror stories are largely due to the excesses of breeding.

The Marks Of A Healthy Cat

It goes without saying that when choosing a cat, you must make sure it's healthy. A healthy cat is active, alert, and curious. Its eyes are clear and bright, the coat is soft, glossy, and clean. If you are taking in a stray cat don't be discouraged if the fur is dirty and stiff. In the clean comfort of your home, and with the benefits provided by a healthy diet, your stray will soon sport a lustrous coat.

A tamed stray can make an excellent pet. To give a stray cat a home is an enormously humane gesture and the spiritual rewards of restoring the cat to a state of good health and original beauty make good lifetime memories.

Preparing For The New Pet

If you acquire your cat spontaneously, meaning that he just walks in the door one day, or follows you home from the store, or charms you into bringing it home, then you may have to complete the preparations suggested below while the cat is in your possession.

Confine the newcomer to the bathroom or a small area in the house that you have made safe. If you have other cats, it is essential to their health that this newest family member be quarantined to separate food, litter facilities, and living quarters until he or she is found to be in good health by the veterinarian.

If this is your first cat, you must "cat-proof" your home. Devise storage facilities that keep pins, rubber bands, strings, and paper clips out of the reach of your pet. It is exceedingly dangerous for cats to play with strings and rubber bands. They can strangle the cat or become dangerously entangled in the animal's intestines causing constipation, internal bleeding, or death. If you find your cat with part of a swallowed string hanging out of its mouth, do not pull the string. Rush the animal to the veterinarian. Paper clips, pins, and tacks can puncture the intestines or stomach of a cat who accidentally swallows them.

Installing The New Cat

Transport the cat to your home in a well-ventilated cat carrier. Cat carriers can be purchased at pet stores and variety stores. Place the cat carrier near a clean litter box. Wait a few minutes before opening it. The confinement provides the cat with a certain amount of security. Allow the cat to sit in the carrier, adjusting to the new smells. The acute feline sense of smell may be overwhelmed by all the new odors. Avoid bringing the cat into a noisy atmosphere. Cats respond well to soft music. Speak to the cat in a soothing, loving voice from a safe but visible distance.

When the cat appears relaxed, tell it that you are going to open the door. Use slow, deliberate movements. Rest your hand lightly on the door, and give the cat a chance to take a few sniffs. Open the door gently and step back, giving the cat ample space. As soon as the cat steps out of the carrier onto the floor gently place it in the litter box. The cat will probably jump out. Put the cat back in but do not restrain it. Do this several times.

If you are bringing the cat home for the first time—straight from the initial visit to the veterinarian—after placing the cat in the litter box, let her calmly explore the environment and discover the feeding place. Give the cat thirty to forty minutes to eat, then remove and clean the food dish. Keep fresh water available.

Making The Adjustment

You and your cat will need some time to adjust to the new living arrangement. The cat will need to get used to the new environment, using its sense of smell to investigate and to decipher. You will need to adjust to your new daily chores involving cat care. Both of you will need to study the other's makeup as you seek a comfortable, loving relationship. It is imperative for you to remain gentle, kind, and calm. Restrain yourself from reaching out to the cat: your cat will seek you out, cuddle up, climb onto your lap, rest a head on your thigh, or rub against your leg, and purr loudly. With a little patience and a lot of attention you will soon be able to relax into many years of companionable contentment.

Bonding By Food And Water

You have probably heard a lot about the independent nature of cats. This "I do my own thing" behavior is a crucial part of what makes them so dramatically attractive. To strengthen your bond with one of nature's most splendid creatures, make sure your cat knows you are responsible for food and water. Fresh water should always be available. Don't just give the cat food, make eating a ritual the cat will really enjoy. You can train the cat by closely adhering to a schedule. Routine is an essential element of a contented feline's lifestyle. So, establish a feeding routine at once.

Naming The Pet

Cats can be trained to answer to a particular name when an affectionate and faithful relationship exists between the cat and its owner. Repeat the cat's name during games, meals, and loving encounters.

Choosing A Veterinarian

Just as you should have a doctor, your cat should have a veterinarian. An excellent means of acquiring a list of reputable veterinarians in your area is by contacting Friends Of Animals. FOA is a national organization that offers low-cost certificates for neutering. Write Friends Of Animals at

P.O. 1244, Norwalk, CT 06856 or call 1-800-631-2212 and ask FOA to send you their literature.

Note the registry of participating vets conveniently listed by county and state. Select two or three that are nearby. These veterinarians, by accepting the FOA certificates, have distinguished themselves as being sensitive to the well-being of animals, and have put the needs of the animals above their own profit motives. Ask friends and relatives what they know about your first choices. A good reputation is important. Telephone the veterinarians and explain that you are about to become (or have just become) the proud new owner of a cat.

What To Look For

Request a tour of the offices. On your tour of the vet's facilities, look for cleanliness, order, and gentleness in handling the animals. Do the doctors and attendants exhibit a soothing, loving concern? Or, are they indifferent and cold? Is the equipment modern and are the treatment areas spotlessly clean?

Notice the smell. Is the aroma offensive? Does it imply a lack of care and cleanliness? Are sedated animals, who have just come out of surgery, immediately placed in clean, well-ventilated, warm cages supplied with food, water, and litter? Are animals left lying around on tables or on the cold floor waiting for attention? Does the staff appear competent and willing to answer your questions? Good communication is key to all medical care including that of your cat's.

Notice the cages the animals are kept in. Do they appear clean and comfortable? The cages of cats and dogs should be separated. If your cat could need overnight attention, you do not want the nerve-wracking experience to be exacerbated by an aggressive dog whose cage is thoughtlessly placed next to your cat.

While experts agree that the ideal is to take your cat to the vet before bringing it home for the first time, they also agree that you should not deny a homeless cat a home by rigidly enforcing this rule.

Providing A Safe Environment

You have heard of child-proofing a home. That is, keeping dangerous obejcts out of the way of the innocent, curious, unsuspecting child. You must also make your home safe for your cat. More injuries occur to cats who have fallen from unscreened windows than any other single hazard. All windows must be securely screened so that your cat will not experience an unnecessary and injurious plunge. Many animal shelters that put cats up for adoption require all windows in the home of the prospective owner to be screened before the cat is released.

Perhaps you are asking why so much fuss over screened windows. Don't cats have perfect balance? While it's true that cats rarely lose their footing, they can receive broken bones and internal injuries from a fall.

You might think that screens are unnecessary if you only open the window slightly. A determined cat can work its head through very small openings. Whatever a cat can get its head through, it can get its body through.

Your cat may try to get at flying prey or follow some irresistible aroma. The result of these falls are broken limbs and bones, internal injuries, and death. Balconies should be closed off so that your cat cannot gain access.

You may decide to open your window from the top rather than invest in screens to protect your pet. Remember the climbing instinct of all cats and the potential head first plunge. The results could be deadly.

Watch out for your cat when opening doors that lead to the outside. *Do not allow your cat access to busy streets.*

Although cats who live in quiet residential districts greatly enjoy backyards and freely roam the neighborhood, crossing streets should be discouraged.

Another hazard for cats is the possibility of being struck by a vehicle in the streets. Cats who are allowed to roam freely stand a good chance of being injured or killed in an automotive accident.

Your Cat's Habits Will Change Yours

These former tree dwellers have retained their climbing instinct. They will climb to the top of a closet or cabinet for a nap. Pay attention when closing closet doors, or shutting drawers. You do not want to come home from work to discover that your beloved pet has been shut up in the refrigerator, closet, or under the kitcken sink all day, away from water and the litter box. In the case of a drawer, there just might not be enough oxygen to sustain the cat's life and the refrigerator is probably the worst case scenario.

Toxic Worries

The fumes from moth balls are deadly. They can destroy the cat's liver cells. You do not want to shut your cat in a closet laced with this deadly poison. Make sure to secure all closets and drawers containing moth crystals so that they are completely inaccessible to your cat.

Put poisons and other toxic substances out of your cat's reach. You do not want your cat to ingest common household items such as dishwashing liquids, laundry detergents, and other cleaning compounds. Cats are highly susceptible to toxic reactions from phenol, an ingredient found in Lysol. Ingestion of these substances by a cat can be fatal. Store all chemical substances in a cat-proofed place.

Healthy cats, especially kittens, are active and curious. They will knock over bottles and boxes as they romp playfully. An insatiable curiosity drives our feline friends to inspect nearly everything in their environment. Avoid leaving harmful or dangerous substances where your cat might accidentally spill them, get some on his fur, lick himself, and, consequently, swallow the poison trying to get clean.

Now that you have a natural mousetrap you will never need to use rat poison. Insect poisons are deadly and dangerous. Use insect traps that your cat cannot get into.

CHAPTER THREE

Be Natural

In our effort to do what is most natural for our cats, we have spent a good deal of time trying to understand how they do things themselves, when living in their natural habitat. We often watch nature documentaries or read books that discuss the habits of the wilderness cats as we look for more insight into the domesticated variety. These animals are closely related and have very similar habits. In trying to decide what to do for your cat, think natural. Consider what the animal would do if it lived in the wilderness and try to approximate that as closely as you can.

Follow Two Natural Rules

There are two cardinal rules to follow assiduously when dealing with your cat:

1. Remember the wild and try to do what is most natural

2. Always be gentle with your cat.

Cats Get Into Everything

Your cat will like what you like. Which means that it will get into everything. That hand-washed sweater, re-shaped and spread on a hard surface to dry, may suddenly acquire paw tracks. Or you may find your cat sleeping in the middle of your just-washed sweater, or attempting to repose dead center in the book or paper that you are reading. In cases like this, remove your cat gently, lovingly, firmly, and say, "No." Remember, yelling at and hitting a cat are repugnant actions. A firm "No" will do the trick.

Size and Intelligence

The average full grown cat is approximately 20" in length from the head to the base of the tail bone. The tail itself is usually 10 to 12 inches long. The average weight of a tomcat is seven to nine lbs; females are from five to seven lbs.

Although small in size, cats are respected for their vivacious intelligence, clever behavior, and brave de-meanor. The cat's courage, however, triumphs over a basically scary nature. Try, always, to keep in mind how vulnerable your little pussycat must feel at the feet of people. Always remain gentle and calm in your cat's presence.

Cats Are Very Sensitive

They are startled by loud noises, harsh voices, and sudden moves. They can sense when you are sad, happy, worried, or nervous. Cats tend to be disturbed when their owners show anxiety. Never yell at your cat or make loud noises to get her attention. When approaching your feline friend speak in soft, soothing, loving tones, reassuring the cat that you mean no harm. When reaching for a cat, keep your hands in sight and reach out to the cat with just one hand.

The Litter Box

During their wilderness days, cats eliminated and buried their excrement at a safe distance from the lair, to avoid revealing their trail to predators. This ancient instinct is carefully followed by healthy house cats today. Cats do not like to have their food placed near the litter box. Some cats adjust. But food near waste is definitely not as the cat would arrange it.

When we were primarily an agrarian society, domestic cats had the great out-of-doors to do their business in. As we became largely city dwellers, the sandbox or shredded newspapers replaced the backyard. Today litter pans make it extremely convenient to care for a cat's toilet needs. Most supermarkets offer a variety of litter. Use any shallow pan from four to five inches deep, and approximatley 18 inches wide. Cover the bottom of the litter pan with two inches of litter.

Clean Litter Is Essential To Your Cat's Sensibility

Cats are happiest when the litter is scooped clean everyday. Remove all feces and wet clumps of urine daily. If you have several cats you may need to clean the litter several times a day. Add enough clean litter to replace what was removed during cleaning.

Three or four times a week, depending upon the disposition of your pussycat, but never less than twice, completely dispose of the old litter, and wash the pan in scalding hot water. Dry it completely and refill with fresh litter. Do not use soaps and cleansers to wash the pan, these substances are toxic and harmful. However, if your cats have recently been treated for an infectious disease, use chlorine bleach to sterilize the litter pan.

Do not add deodorizers or antiseptics to litter. Keep it natural. The litter you choose, clay, green alfalfa pellets, sawdust, cedar chips, or shredded paper, depends upon you and your cat. Use a brand that has not been treated with any additives or deodorizers. You do not want your cat to expose herself to chemicals that might not agree with her. Natural is safest. The best deodorizer is daily cleaning.

Cats who are maintained on a healthy diet, groomed regularly, and whose owners keep scrupulously clean litter pans, tend not to excrete offensive odors.

Separating Kitten From Mother
Leave the kitten with its mother until it is two months old. A two-month-old will have learned valuable how-to-be-a-good-cat lessons from its mother. It will also have had the benefit of the mother's nourishing milk.

Do not worry about the kitten missing its mother or siblings. The little tyke will forget them in a matter of hours and quickly adjust to the new environment. Transport the kitten in a carrier.

Play Is Important
The rambunctious, playful kitten must be taught how to live in a house with people. Kittens and many adult cats will run out of a door as soon as it is opened. Since kittens have not yet learned how to keep their claws in sheath when playing, it is best not to suddenly approach them with caresses. In fact, never suddenly approach any cat. Always announce your intentions to the cat. Use a consistent form of communication. Offer affection only when the kitten spontaneously approaches you, and be careful that it doesn't scratch.

The constant playing of a kitten is essential to the

growth of dexterity and intelligence. It should be encouraged.

Cats Tire Easily

Cats tire more quickly than dogs and are not generally disposed to taking walks or running. Cats tend to get their exercise in short bursts of activity, playfully stalking prey.

If you plan to use a leash, to take your cat walking, discuss this practice with your vet. Keep the walks short and minimize the stress potential.

Respect The Cat's Need To Nap

Healthy, contented cats prefer to sleep 14 to 16 hours per day. A reposing cat can snap awake instantly. These naps are often interrupted as the cat moves from one favored sleeping place to another. Your cat will spend a great deal of time napping, or sitting in quiet solitude. It is natural for a cat.

Discourage A Wandering Cat

Displaying a remarkable sense of orientation, many cats have overcome long and difficult distances to come again to affection and fidelity. Their native instinct propels most cats to wander. However, neutered cats are less likely to wander far than a cat driven by the sexual instinct to reproduce.

Most cats who have free access to the out of doors will wander—some briefly, others at length. Some cats routinely spend two or three days at a time away from home. Such freedom of movement is dangerous. The cat can become the victim of an accident, a vicious fight, or an encounter with an individual who hates cats enough to harm them. Also, if a cat gets far enough from home, even his potent orientation will not bring him back. If he is exceedingly beautiful, he may be stolen. If you insist on letting your cat roam, at least equip the vulnerable feline with an indentification collar that contains your name and telephone number.

CHAPTER FOUR

Feed Your Cat A Nutritious Diet

A nutritious, high-quality diet is the best way to assure a healthy, happy cat. Your cat's freedom from sickness, disease, obesity, and a poor disposition is the owner's responsibility.

Instinctively carnivorous in its wild state, the feline feeds on living prey—mice, birds, snakes, frogs, crickets, and other small animals—which provides complete nutrition. Domestic cats, probably as a result of their contact with human beings, are often omnivores unlike the lynx, lion, and tiger, who remain strictly carnivorous. To achieve a balanced diet while living among human beings, domestic cats enjoy meat, dairy, and many green plants.

The Importance Of A Properly Balanced Diet

For the last several years, Americans have been sternly warned by the medical establishment that our meat-centered diets are out of balance, and that heart disease, hypertension, diabetes, and cancer are direct results of an imbalanced diet. This is a warning that "health nuts" have been issuing for decades. Like their human friends, cats require a balanced diet that supplies all of their nutritional requirements. Determine a menu and feeding schedule that works well for your lifestyle and your pussycat's nutritional needs. Plan a routine that guarantees your cat all of the protein, minerals, and vitamins that will keep her healthy, alert, and sporting a beautiful coat with a bright sheen.

Cats Like To Know What To Expect

Observe your cat's eating habits. From this you become aware of what and how much food the cat needs. Although healthy cats will usually regulate their food intake, many cats will eat too much. Beware of feeding your cat to the point of obesity. Never leave food out for your cat to nibble on all day.

Perhaps you have had your cat for a while and are just getting around to reading this book. You may discover the need to make some changes in your cat's diet to attain the standards presented here. Some cats will easily make the change, others will stubbornly refuse the new foods and cling to the old. Use a gradual approach. Over a period that does not exceed a month, mix the new food with the old. Begin with small amounts and gradually increase the ratio until, by the end of the month, there is no trace of the old food. If the cat refuses a few meals during the adjustment period, don't worry. He will eventually become hungry enough to eat the new food.

Feeding Kittens

As stated earlier, a kitten should not be taken from its mother before it is two months old. During this critical growth period, the kitten receives a balanced high-quality diet through its mother's milk. Between eight and ten weeks, functioning in accordance with nature's built-in calendar, the mother weans the kittens. Like babies, kittens need to eat several times a day. The caloric requirements of the active kitten are higher than an adult cat's. Your kitten will, depending upon its age, size, healthiness, and activity, consume three to seven ounces per day of meat, rice, milk, cheese, raw and steamed vegetables.

A kitten between the ages of two to five months should be fed a tablespoonful of food four times a day. The best brands of cat food offer formulas specifically designed for growing kittens.

At five months, another weaning must occur: The number of meals the kitten consumes should be reduced to three. From eight to twelve months give your kitten two meals per day.

Fish

The feline love of fish is well known. It is a delicacy that cats adore, and you should use it only periodically as a main course. Do not serve fish instead of meat as a staple. You will achieve greater nutritional balance when you use beef as the staple, offering chicken, eggs, fish, and organ meats as supplements. Just as you do not make regular meals of delicacies, do not train your cat to do so.

Avoid serving tuna because it is excessively high in fat content. Tuna is also implicated in kidney stones. Remove all bones from fish before serving it to your cat or kitten.

Meat Is The Main Course

Meat is the staple of a cat's diet, although some owners have trained their cats to eat a vegetarian diet. If you prefer not to use canned meat that comes in commercially-prepared cat food, you may cook beef, chicken, and fish for your cat. Although cats eat their prey raw, do not feed your cat raw meat. The prey is absolutely fresh. Butchered meat accumlates germs that are killed in the cooking process. It may also contain parasites.

Remove all bones from any meat you cook for your cat. Never feed bones of any kind to your cat. Bones can splinter, get lodged in the cat's teeth, mouth, throat, or digestive tract, and cause serious harm. Bones, however, contain valuable nutrients. You can select a brand of commercial food that includes bone meal. Another option is to purchase bone meal and add it to your cat's food on a regular basis.

Avoid all pork, but especially processed meats such as ham, lunch meat, sausage, and hot dogs. All of these products contain additives that can accumulate in your cat's system and result in disease.

The Nutritional Needs of Felines

Protein is very important to good nutrition. Cats digest animal proteins easily and tend to prefer them. Soy, wheat germ, and yeast are plant proteins that are healthy supplements.

Carbohydrates are an excellent source of energy for your cat. Cereals and starchy vegetables are excellent sources of carbohydrates. Serve them cooked. Green leafy vegetables, in small amounts, can be served raw. Allow your cat to instinctively choose what is good for him.

Vitamins

The vitamins and their sources listed below are essential to proper growth and good health.

Vitamin	Source
A	Liver, eggs, fish and fish liver oils, green and yellow vegetables, milk

Vitamin	Source
B-1	Muscle and organ meats, eggs, grains, yeast, yellow vegetables, and milk
B-2	Liver, vegetables, yeast
B complex	Muscle and organ meats, yeast, milk, vegetables
C	Manufactured by the cat's body from glucose
D	Fish, fish liver oils, eggs
E	Liver, cereals, wheat germ

The Big Four

Folic Acid and Vitamin B-12 help produce your cat's vital red blood cells. A deficiency of either of these essential elements will cause anemia. Biotin produces healthy skin. It also tones the cat's circulatory system. The feline metabolism, bones, teeth, and healing process are dependent upon adequate ingestion of Vitamin C. A properly balanced, high-quality diet should require little supplementation of these important nutrients. It is advisable, however, to supplement them when your cat is facing or recovering from an illness or surgery.

Keep A Balance

While Vitamin C is a vital nutrient to a well-balanced cat diet, excessive amounts may result in the formation of kidney stones.

A delicate balance needs to be maintained in getting nutrients into the cat's system. Too little or too much can hurt the cat.

Taurine

A total lack of this amino acid in a cat's diet can result in blindness. Muscle meat such as beef or chicken usually provides ample quantities.

Supplements

Toasted wheat germ and brewers or nutritional yeast greatly enhance the cat's diet. The wheat germ offers roughage and aids elimination, while it is a powerful source of nutrition. Yeast is an excellent source of the B vitamins. Even if you select a brand of cat food that includes wheat germ and yeast in the list of ingredients, serve a half-teaspoon of wheat germ, per cat, and a teaspoon of yeast per cat, per day. Mix the yeast and wheat germ with the cat's regular portion. Several times each week, add a half-teaspoon of fish liver oil to your cat's meal. At other times add a dash of bone meal.

Beware Of Too Much Fat In Your Cat's Diet

Fats are essential for a healthy coat and skin. Nevertheless, the fatty intake of your cat's diet should never exceed 40 percent. To do so, puts your beloved pet at risk of obesity, lethargy, clogged blood vessels, and heart disease. Activity and agility are natural elements of a well-rounded cat personality. An overfed cat, slowed and clogged by excessive eating, is less than happy.

How Much Is Enough?

There are many influences on the amount that your cat will eat. Breed, weight, height, activity, and stress are some of the factors. You will need to study your cat's eating patterns to determine what is right for him. An adult cat can be fed two small meals per day or one abundant meal in the evening. Some experts recommend a healthy table-spoonful of food per cat per meal, while others recommend that a cat be allowed to eat as much he or she wants for no more than a half an hour. Do not make the mistake of overfeeding your adult cat. It is less active than the kitten and requires fewer calories.

An active, healthy neutered adult cat weighing eight pounds consumes between five to seven ounces of food per day. By contrast, a healthy, active, growing two-pound kitten between ten and 20 weeks of age requires approximately seven ounces of canned food per day.

A physically and psychologically healthy cat will tend to regulate its own level of consumption when all of the required nutrients are sufficiently provided.

Break The Milk Myth

After weaning—eight to ten weeks—cats do not need milk. Most cats lack the proper bacteria to digest milk and suffer diarrhea when too much milk is included in the diet. Milk should be used cautiously in an adult cat's diet; serve it occasionally in small portions.

Maintain Quality Control

If you are uncertain about the quality of your cat's diet, discuss it with your veterinarian. Ask whether you need to add a quality vitamin supplement to enhance your pet's diet while you take the needed steps to bring it in line with the cat's nutritional requirements.

To achieve a balanced diet offer your cat a variety of food on a regular basis. Variety does not mean a daily change, it means a combining of the required nutrients in one plate of food. An excellent diet will protect the cat from disease and provide the fuel to fight off infections.

By-Products

Avoid pre-prepared cat food that uses by-products. Intestines, veins, eyes, and bones, which the cat would consume if he stalked and captured live prey, have nutritional value. They are not by-products in cat food. By-products are wastes that are considered too toxic for human consumption. So let's consider them to be dangerous to our pets.

Ash

Avoid feeding your cat a high-ash diet. Dry foods are highest in ash content. Fish products also contain large amounts of ash. Indications are that magnesium, a component of the ash found in dry cat food, is a main contributing factor in crystal formation in cat urine. This disorder leads to kidney and bladder stones and clogged urinary tracts. Select a low-ash, low magnesium canned meat as the main course of your cat's nutrition.

Read All Labels

Avoid brands that list preservatives such as BHA, BHT, food coloring, and artificial flavorings among the ingredients.

Supermarkets and pet stores offer a wide variety of commercial brands to choose from.

When selecting a brand of cat food look for ingredients such as beef, water, rice, eggs, cheese, liver, soy flour, chicken, lecithin, taurine, yeast, wheat germ, dried kelp, vitamin supplements including A, B, D, and E.

Table Scraps Are A Good Cat Food Source

For centuries, domestic cats have been fed table scraps. It is a viable alternative. If you feed your cat table scraps, do not offer food covered with gravy, sauces, spices, and bones. It is advisable to add yeast, chopped steamed vegetables, fish liver oil and eggs to your cat's portion of meat on a regular basis. Do not serve ham or pork. Pork is excessively fatty.

Many cats, although they cannot stomach milk, enjoy cheese. Cereals, rice, pasta and wheat, used sparingly, will enhance your cat's nutrition. Avoid giving these high caloric foods to a fat cat.

Plants and Vegetables

Cats who live outside enjoy nibbling and grazing, especially in grassy areas. Cats who live indoors reflect this habit by eating house plants. This is dangerous since numerous house plants are harmful to cats. If your cat shows a disposition for green things, offer the cat bits of raw vegetables. You may also cultivate several pots of grass for your cat. Grass is an excellent digestive aid that induces the passage of the inevitable hair balls.

Feeding Utensils

If you own more than one cat, each of them should have a separate plate for eating. After each feeding remove and wash the food plates. Use hot water and a clean dish cloth you have reserved for the cat's dishes. Do not use dishwashing liquids on your cat's plate. Hot water and a good scrubbing cleans the utensils of a healthy cat and protects the cat's system from bacteria and toxic substances.

Water

Serve a separate bowl of water for every three cats. Use a shallow bowl with a depth of no more than two or three inches and a diameter of five to six inches.

Serve Your Cat's Food At Room Temperature

Serve your cat's food at room temperature, never hot or directly from the refrigerator. Avoid warming food more than once. Each time it is warmed it becomes more susceptible to invasion by harmful bacteria.

If you maintain a busy schedule and like to store a two-or-three day supply in the refrigerator, use a jar for each day.

Never Leave Food For Your Cat Out Longer
Than An Hour!

Remove and wash the food plates within one hour of feeding, even if your cat did not eat. Discard leftovers. You can try again at the next meal time. Your cat may be taking an instinctive, system-cleansing fast. Food left out may interfere with this process as the scent will spur the cat's digestive juices into action and perhaps force him to eat when his instincts say no.

There are owners who replenish the empty bowl as soon as it becomes empty. Few of nature's creatures eat constantly or experience the aroma of their favorite food constantly. To do so is to distort the appetite and to blunt the sense of smell. If you leave food down throughout the day your cat will probably overeat, become fat, lethargic and die prematurely.

The cat's appetite is stimulated by its sense of smell. The constant availability of the smell of his food, even while the cat has a full stomach, also results in finicky, non-eating behavior.

Older Cats

As your cat grows older and becomes less active, her food needs will also change. Older cats should be served very small pieces of meat or soft cheese.

Use Small Amounts Of Dry Food

Controversy rages over dry food or canned meat food. Most agree, however, that the moist foods, are of generally poor quality. Dry food advocates claim it is needed for cleaning the cat's teeth. Canned meat advocates point to dry food's high ash content. Avoid moist foods altogether as they may not provide a balanced diet.

The Ideal Choice

For busy owners who choose not to use table scraps or cook for their cat, canned cat foods are the ideal choice. They are highest in moisture and nutritional content, and lowest in ash. Veterinarians advise avoiding brands which list an ash content over 4.0 percent. Other experts claim ash should be kept below 3.0 percent.

Buy the cat's food by the case—it is more economical. To guarantee freshness do not stock more than one month's supply.

No Raw Meat!

Never feed the cat raw meat. It may contain harmful bacteria or parasites. You may serve the cat small amounts of cooked organ meats (liver, kidneys, and hearts).

You and your cat will determine what and how much the cat eats. Follow the guidelines for a balanced diet offered above and the natural inclinations of your feline friend.

CHAPTER FIVE

Know Your Cat's Inoculations, Signs Of Sickness, And Dangerous Diseases

When it comes to the inoculations that your cat needs, the cliche "an ounce of prevention is worth a pound of cure" should be observed.

If you have not already done so, make an appointment for an immediate visit to the veterinarian. What a tragedy it is to lose a beloved pet to a disease that she can be inoculated against.

Ebony, a sleek jet black tom, lived with Ron since he was a kitten. Soon after Ron bought the small house he lived in, he adopted Ebony. They were a family. When Ron was home, he and Ebony were constant companions. In a few months he taught the graceful feline how to fetch and retrieve objects. These dog-like activities are rare in cats. Ebony was special.

Suddenly, Ron noticed that Ebony was losing weight. Then he noticed that he was eating less food and soon exhibited no appetite at all. It was time to go to the veterinarian. The diagnosis was shocking: Ebony had contracted the lethal feline leukemia. The veterinarian informed Ron that he had a major decision to make. He said that Ebony would suffer immensely. Predicting a rapidly declining state, familiar with the horror of slow death, the veterinarian recommended immediate euthanasia. He told Ron that each day would see a worsening in the poor cat's condition. All his feline pride, dignity, and innate cleanliness would be lost to the virus.

Ron took Ebony home and nursed him tenderly for three days. Sadly, he recognized the precision of the doctor's prognosis—each day Ebony's condition worsened. Ron was heartbroken when he saw the once agile and powerful tom so weak that he could not climb into the litter box. Unwilling to see the beautiful animal suffer anymore, he made an appointment with the veterinarian and stayed with Ebony through the end.

Ron was devastated by the death of his beloved cat. His deep sense of loss was greatly exacerbated by the knowledge that Ebony could still be with him had he not followed the advice of a friend and delayed getting the feline leukemia shot when he got Ebony's other inoculations.

The Important Innoculations

There are six vaccinations your cat must have. They are discussed below.

Distemper—Feline Panleucopenia (FPL) is a highly common and contagious disease. It destroys white blood cells. Because this dangerous virus is resistant to disinfectants, it is a powerful adversary of your cat, capable of surviving for long periods of time around your home. Even if your cat is an apartment dweller who never goes outside, she risks an FPL infection. Anyone can step on something outside that is contaminated and carry it into the house.

FPL is fatal and can strike without warning. Young cats can be found dead without showing any previous signs of illness. When cats do show symptoms, they act depressed, refuse to eat, and vomit. This deadly virus attack the bone marrow and intestinal linings of a kitten. It also destroys the liver, spleen and lymph nodes of an adult cat. Although the animal becomes severely dehydrated, the poor little creature can only sit and stare at her water bowl. The kitty also feels cold and rigid, and will cry out in pain when touched.

Since there isn't any treatment that offers a good likelihood of successful recovery, the mortality rate is high. Most cats with FPL are put to sleep to spare them the eventual pain and misery associated with the final stages of the disease. Although kittens are more susceptible, this extremely contagious viral disease attacks cats of all ages. Get your pet vaccinated against this deadly killer.

Feline Rhinotracheitis and **Feline Calicivirus** are two viruses that strike the upper respiratory system in cats. The cat can get puffy eyes with discharge, sinusitis, ulcers in the mouth and have difficulty breathing. Many, many kittens die of this disease. With aggressive therapy, some can be saved, but their growth is stunted and the suffering they go through is terrible. Get your cat vaccinated against this nasty infection.

Feline Pneumonitis attacks the cat's upper respiratory system. It is one of the few diseases that is transmissible between cats and people. It causes your cat to suffer severe swelling of the eyes that is accompanied by itchiness. Although Feline Pneumonitis can be treated successfully, it takes weeks for most cats to get over the infection.

There is no effective antiviral drug for these upper respiratory viral diseases. Cats must recover from respiratory infection using their own natural defense mechanisms.

A cat with a good immune system can usually recover from the ravaging infection. But upper respiratory tract viruses weaken the body, making it susceptible to secondary bacteria. A cat under treatment by a veterinarian for upper respiratory infection should be administered antibiotics to prevent this further invasion of the cat's sick body. Get this important inoculation for your cat.

Rabies is not considered much of a problem anymore because dogs and cats are routinely vaccinated against it. Recently, however, heavily populated states such as New Jersey and New York have reported numerous cases. Rabies is always fatal. Mice, rats, and squirrels carry rabies. Rabies is a deadly killer. Protect your cat against it.

Feline Leukemia (FeLV) is now a well-known, dreaded killer. It is a retrovirus that causes cancer, among other things. Similar to human AIDS, FeLV strikes at the immune system. It can remain dormant for years. Many cats have carried the latent form of the virus only to develop tumors late in life.

Your cat can be exposed to this deadly killer by coming in contact with the contaminated saliva, urine, or feces of an infected cat. It can also be transmitted by fleas or ticks.

Although there is no cure for FeLV, there is a vaccination that is almost 100 percent effective in preventing FeLV in cats not carrying the virus. Feline Leukemia, when it strikes, is devastating, and causes a slow death, with one body system failing after another.

Immunizing Against Infectious Diseases Is A Major Priority

A properly immunized mother cat will pass valuable immunity on to her kittens during the nursing period. Kittens should be immunized as soon as they are weaned.

Immunity is never permanent. All antibodies subside

over time. To adequately protect your cat from infectious disease, the vaccinations should be repeated yearly.

Vaccinations are usually performed on the cat's first visit to the veternarian. Depending upon your locale the cost of these inoculations may vary from $25.00 to $35.00. In some instances the vaccinations are included in the cost of the office visit.

Kittens will ideally get their first set of inoculations at age six weeks, with booster shots following at nine weeks, twelve weeks and six months.

Temperature

A cat's normal temperature is 100°-102° F. An elevated temperature is a sure sign of sickness. The only way to be completely certain of the state of your cat's body temperature is to take it with a thermometer. Lubricate the thermometer with petroleum jelly.

Have someone hold the cat's head and front legs while you lift the cat's tail and gently push the thermometer into the rectum. Insert it about one inch into the anus. Never force the thermometer! If you are unable to take the temperature easily do not aggravate the cat's stress level by forcing the issue. Take your cat to the veterinarian.

Know The Signs Of Sickness

There is body language that you can look for to tell if your cat is feeling bad. Many cats fast intermittently. The average fast lasts two or three days, with long ones extending to a week. If your cat stops eating for more than two or three days, or exceeds its usual fasting pattern, look for other signs of sickness. If you are aware your cat has a pattern for fasting, when the non-eating behavior extends beyond that period look for signs of sickness. Refusal to eat is one of the first indications of illness.

A cat who is listless, sleeps more than usual, has red eyes, or a dull coat is probably sick and in need of medical attention. If vomiting, coughing or diarrhea persist take the cat to the vet at once.

A drastic change in behavior, habits, appetite, a different way of walking, resting in strange positions, excessive restlessness, disinterest in things that it normally likes, and not using the litter box may indicate that your cat is sick. Healthy cats often seek quiet solitude; an ill cat will seek a hiding place to nurse itself back to good health.

Not all changes require a trip to the veterinarian. Knowing your cat's habits lets you make adjustments based on what the cat communicates.

Provide Roughage And Aid The Prevention of Constipation

Middle-aged and old-aged, overweight cats often suffer from chronic constipation. If left untreated it can result in death. The colons of these little creatures are clogged by impacted fecal matter. Cats who get little exercise are most at risk. A cat with a routine that consists mostly of eating and sleeping, who only moves his bowels once every three or four days, is badly constipated. A severe case of constipation can require hospitalization for treatment that includes warm water enemas, and oral medication. In the worst cases, the doctor will have to remove the impacted feces surgically. This procedure, which requires anesthesia, is extremely stressful and exhausting for the cat.

A Variety Of Worms Attack Cats

The most common worm infestations occur in the cat's intestinal tract. But there are parasites that invade the cat's heart, lungs, liver, and even the eyes. Worms get into the cat's system through the mouth or from flea, tick or mosquito bites.

There are many types of worms that can infest a cat's body and each requires a different treatment. It takes the well-trained eye of a veterinarian to identify the numerous types. Make it a routine practice to take a stool sample along when you take your cat to the vet.

You can greatly aid the prevention of worms if you feed your cat only cooked food and keep the litter box clean. Do not try to treat a case of worms yourself with over-the-counter medication. It might not kill the worms and it may be harmful to your cat. Consult your veterinarian if you suspect worms.

Signs and Symptoms

The coat of infected cats is dry and dull. Dry coughing, chronic hacking, lethargy, loss of appetite, diarrhea, constipation, a potbelly, and emaciation may be a sign of worms. A lack of weight gain while eating huge amounts of food, and chronic or bloody diarrhea may also signal that parasites are infesting your cat.

If you think your cat has worms consult your veterinarian. Appropriate treatment will get rid of them.

Mites Are Parasites, Too

Ear mites live in the outer canal of your cat's ear. If you notice a brown-black, waxy discharge, your cat probably has ear mites. You can treat a mild infestation with over-the-counter preparations. A severe infestation will require the assistance of a veterinarian to flush out the layers of mites and wax. The treatment is extended over a two-month period because ear mite eggs take up to two months to hatch.

Head mange or crusty scaly patches of dandruff, accompanied by vigorous scratching, are signs of microscopic mite infestation. There are several very effective commercial treatments for this disorder. Ask your veterinarian to recommend a treatment plan. Most of the treatments for flaky dandruff can be very toxic if overused.

Fleas

These tiny insects love warm-blooded animals. But they prefer to live on animals with fur. The bite of this tiny bloodsucker results in intense irritation. The problem is worsened as the cat scratches the irritated area seeking relief.

If your cat has fleas ask your vet to recommend a nontoxic, organic flea treatment. Always give the cat a bath following the treatment.

The sturdy flea can survive formidable extermination efforts. To conquer this invader completely, the cat's owner must unleash an all-out assault designed to kill all stages of the flea's life cycle. To achieve flea control your extermination plan must include all the places in the house where a flea or flea eggs might hide.

The best flea control products are accompanied by a dip that the cat is immersed in. Discuss with your veterinarian the best plan for eradicating fleas. The odds are against a well-nourished cat getting fleas, especially if the cat is getting brewers yeast, and is groomed regularly.

Ticks

Ticks are a bloodsucking parasite with a hearty appetite. They cause anemia in cats. Any good commercial flea or tick spray or powder will rid your cat of ticks.

Lice

Lice burrow into the cat's skin, and are easily spread from one infected animal to another. These sharp-clawed animals cause intense irritation. Shampoo an infected cat once a week for four weeks with an herbal insecticidal pet shampoo.

It is essential to follow carefully all of the directions on any parasite eradication program!

Tumors

Cats can have a range of benign and malignant tumors in nearly all of their body systems. The symptoms are varied and depend on where the tumor is located on the cat's body. Regular check-ups by the vet assure early detection. Early detection is the most important factor in treating tumors.

Poisoned Cats Are The Exception

The particular, fastidious cat does not quickly ingest unfamiliar substances, so that poisoned cats are rare. However poisonings do occur. For centuries angry neighbors have fed troublesome pets poisoned food.

There are numerous plants that cause toxic reactions in cats. These reactions are usually slight, resulting in vomiting. There are numerous pesticides, insecticides, and household chemicals that if ingested by the cat, can cause severe poisoning. If you suspect that your cat has been poisoned, call the veterinarian immediately. Describe the substance and ask for an antidote you can administer to help the cat as you rush the animal, and a sample of the substance, to the veterinarian. Failure to act quickly can result in the death of your pet.

Urinary Tract Disease

Diseases of the urinary tract are numerous, with symptoms running the gamut from a tremendous increase in urination and thirst to a complete absence of urination and thirst. Pronounced pain may be evident over the mid-back region, and the cat may display a hunched back posture. Frequent squatting to urinate is a sure sign of a urinary tract disorder. Often, the urge to urinate will be so intense that the cat will squat before reaching the litter. Other times nothing will come out.

CHAPTER SIX

The Scratching Post Is Important

Scratching is a natural activity for cats. Old nails are removed and new ones are allowed to grow. Cats who live out of doors will scratch tree trunks. Those who live indoors have the same preference for rough scratching surfaces. Providing your cat with a coarse scratching post upon her arrival will save your furniture.

Cats scratch to file their nails and to leave a sign that will be noticed by other cats. It indicates territory and boundaries. Cats are creatures of habit that can be taught to scratch in a specific place.

You Can Make Your Own

If you are unable to obtain a wood scratching post, wrap a rough material such as coarse canvas, burlap, the back side of an old piece of carpet around a 4″ × 4″ post, or a tree branch. Nail it firmly to a sturdy base that will hold the post securely upright against the cat's weight. Your cat will not find a wobbly post very attractive. Allow the cat plenty of stretching and growing room. A sturdy, attractive scratching post is an excellent place for your cat to exercise.

Do not plop the post down in front of your cat. He will probably walk away from the intrusion. When the post is ready for use, spread catnip over it. The cat will come to investigate. If your cat does not seem to catch on immediately, teach her to use the scratching post.

Teach Your Cat How To Use The Scratching Post

Teach a kitten proper scratching behavior by scratching your fingernails against the post. Alternate by gently placing the kitten's paws on the rough surface and moving them in a similar scratching motion. Follow the same procedure with adolescent and adult cats. A cat who has been scratching the furniture for years may find it impossible to alter that long established behavior.

After months of following the method for training kittens, deodorizing the former scratching areas, and perhaps resorting to squirting your little friend in the face with a water pistol, an altered scratching pattern may or may not occur. It is wise to train your cat to a scratching post as early as possible.

Train Your Cat Away From Your Furniture At Once

In the best of circumstances you will have a scratching post in place when the cat arrives. If you do, after the cat has had some nourishment and water, apply the catnip to the post. If you have purchased a post that comes with catnip, keep it well concealed until you are ready for the cat to discover it.

If you are introducing a scratching post to cats already in residence, you will want to train them to use it. Place a scratching post in a secure, permanent location. Many owners provide a scratching post, or scratching areas in several rooms. Others provide a scratching post for each cat since cats are such territorial animals.

Many, many cats are taken in without prior warning. In that case pick a sacrificial place that you do not mind giving over to a cat's scratching. Draw the cat to the prescribed area with the catnip.

A cat conditioned early to a scratching post is far less likely to attack your furniture.

Jenny, a beautiful seal pointe Siamese, was trained to scratch the back of a piece of carpet. When Jenny's claws have made shreds of an old one, a new remnant is introduced. Her master rubs the old piece against the new piece trying to get some of the recognizable scents onto it. He also rubs in catnip to attract Jenny to the new scratching area, which is kept in the same place.

A High Quality Scratching Post

The Katnip Tree made by the Felix Company in Seattle, Washington is a recognized leader in scratching post manufacturing. These sisal covered wooden posts are filled with catnip. Cats are said to cavort with anticipation and joy while the Katnip Tree is still in its wrappings. Many savvy pet store owners now stock the tree. If you are unable to find it call toll free 1-800-24-FELIX and ask for a catalog. The most stubborn feline can be trained away from furniture to this excellent cat product.

Claws Are Integral To Paws

The cat's claws come out of their sheath on command. The front paws have five claws, the rear paws four. Include fondling your cat's paws in your displays of affection. Become familiar with their anatomy. This familiarity will aid both you and the cat when the nails must be trimmed.

Your cat's claws are an essential part of its overall makeup, both physically and psychologically. The claws provide grip which accounts, in part, for the creature's amazing balance. They prevent the cat from slipping and sliding. This ability to grip affords the cat great confidence to climb, run, and jump.

Claws are part of the cat's communication system. Claws out is a warning to stop an unwanted activity. A cat who is freely able to communicate this requirement feels a lot more secure and stress-free than the cat who does not. Cats signal warm feelings by gently kneading with their claws.

Declawing?
If declawing is the only way you will maintain a home for the cat and you have been unable to find another home for him, then declawing is preferable to abandonment. Many veterinarians, however, will not perform the declawing operation because it is unecessary and causes the cat undue pain and suffering.

Take Good Care Of Your Cat's Nails
A healthy cat's nails need trimming every two weeks. Use a human toenail clipper. Clip the nail in the middle of the hook. Stay away from the pinkish core of blood vessels in the cat's nail. If you accidentally cut the vessels, you will hurt the cat and cause bleeding. Apply pressure with a sterile gauze pad to stop the bleeding. Clipping your cat's nails should be a painless procedure accompanied by love and petting.

The Inevitable Scratch
From time to time, over the course of your cat's life, you will experience an accidental scratch. Start early to let your kitten or cat know that scratching you is unacceptable behavior. Be calm, consistent, and firm in your response.

Say no, and immediately stop the activity that brought the claws out.

If you should take in an adult cat with well-established scratching habits, avoid putting yourself in a vulnerable position. It is never a good idea to play games with your cat that put your skin in jeopardy of an accidental scratch. Use toys on strings, or sticks, or throw balls or catnip-filled toy mice away from yourself past the cat. He will be inclined to chase the object. Practice stroking only when your cat offers himself and is in a position that does not readily allow for a scratch. It is unusual for a cat to bite or scratch the hand that feeds her. When it does happen, it is usually an accident caused by exuberant or overly stressful behavior.

If you are scratched by your cat during play, firmly say no and immediately stop the activity. Turn away from and leave the cat. Wash the scratch with an antiseptic. If you are trying to administer medicine, restrain the cat according to the directions given in the section on restraining for medication.

CHAPTER SEVEN

Birth Control

The number of stray and homeless cats is steadily increasing. Experts estimate that for every cat who has a home there are three strays. The problem has become so horrendous that a county in California has passed a law forbidding the birth of cats; the state of Maryland forbids breeding.

The goal is to obtain a lower birth rate. For those of us who love animals and especially cats, this is one way to keep so many of our little friends from suffering the unhappy life of the streets. Cats have a hard time in the streets, or in the abject misery of medical lab research. Cats suffer miserably under experimentation. Let's look at the fate of twelve kittens. Only two kittens per twelve have any chance of finding a good home. Six will be placed in homes where they will eventually be abandoned. Four will be euthanized in a shelter.

Perhaps you are wondering what all this has to do with birth control. A lot.

You may be looking forward to shepherding in your

first litter of newborn kittens and have promises of a home for each of them. People tend to love kittens and want them as pets for themselves and for their small children. But far too often, these same people discover that little kittens and little kids don't always mix well, and that the responsibility is greater than they care to undertake. Before you place a cat or kitten in an adoptive home ask yourself these questions: Can I be sure that the people will take good care of it? Can I be certain that the new owners will feed and water the cat regularly, keep the litter box clean and get it to the vet for regular visits or in emergencies? Can I be sure that these people will not neglect or abuse the animal? Am I certain that the vulnerable feline will not be abandoned?

You might be surprised to learn that many people do not take care of their animals as seriously as you do. Many individuals who are fascinated with kittens get rid of them as soon as they become grown cats, or once they discover how much responsibility caring for a cat entails.

An abandoned cat let loose to fend for itself in the fields or the streets doesn't stand a chance! An enormous expenditure of life occurs as 14 million cats and dogs are put to death within a week of being rescued by a shelter.

Even if you have found excellent homes for the kittens in your litter, what about the next time? Cats breed very fast and you will soon run out of friends and relatives willing to take the kittens. According to the experience of experts: **Cats who have been neutered or spayed make the best pets. They are happier and so are their owners.**

The Drive Of Sex

Although the period of heat varies from cat to cat it can last from a few days to twenty to thirty days in the spring. A female cat can experience the difficult days of heat three or four times a year. Accompanied by a loss of good humor a female in heat wants to be caressed often, rubs her belly on the floor and yowls loudly.

Some owners try to solve the problem by isolating the female during the period of heat. This is generally a very difficult task. A cat who has been allowed to roam freely about her environment will not appreciate being confined for weeks at a time and will react aggressively. Female cats in heat will scratch and call fiercely, day and night, trying to find their mate.

Sexually excited male cats become nervous, lose their appetites and will spray urine marking their territory in an attempt to attract a female in heat. During the period of sexual excitation both male and female cats will scratch, dig, yell, and run out of the first open door or window. An unfixed, unmated cat undergoes horrendous amounts of psychological stress during estrus and according to the experience of experts, if left unchecked over time, this stress can result in disease and a bad personality.

The Benefits Of Spaying And Altering

Female cats who are neutered face much less risk of developing breast cancer or diseases of the uterus. Your male cat will not want to fight with other animals and faces less risk of developing prostate infections or cancer.

The urine of an unneutered male cat will become increasingly strong in odor as the cat matures. If you allow your cat to develop the habit of spraying and the aggressive behavior patterns associated with mating before the surgical alteration occurs, these habits might not be eliminated by surgery. The male cat who is neutered early enough will not develop the spraying habit nor will his urine develop that wild smell.

Experts agree that neutered cats become more calm, affectionate and less inclined to roam. Discuss this important issue with your vet.

When Should I Get My Cat Fixed?

Most cats are ready for neutering between the ages of four to six months. Normally, by this time, their sexual organs are fully developed.

The female cat should not be operated on when in heat. This can cause serious complications.

The male cat should be neutered when his testicles become visible. Avoid having your male cat fixed before his testicles have descended. To do so may result in stunted growth, a weak, whiny voice, a too small head, and weak claws. If your male cat is over four months and you cannot detect testicles, consult your vet. There are cases of undescended testicles.

Until your cat is altered keep him or her close to home. You don't want to be responsible for the production of an unwanted litter and the resulting misery and possible premature death.

Complications from surgical neutering are rare. Modern veterinary has such a low incidence of surgical mishap that the risk of not altering is greater than that presented by surgery. Recovery from the surgery is usually so uneventful that the cat is completely recovered and back to business within a few days.

If you have not followed the advice offered in the beginning of this book to call Friends of Animals for information concerning their low-cost breeding control program, pick up the phone now and dial 1-800-631-2212.

CHAPTER EIGHT

Caring For A Pregnant Cat

A female cat should have a physical examination before she is mated for breeding. However, if the pregnancy is accidental the first sign of pregnancy is pink teats (ordinarily they are very white.) The feline gestation period lasts for nine weeks. Take your cat into the vet for an examination between the fifth and sixth weeks of pregnancy.

Labor can occur as early as the seventh week and as late as the tenth week. However if your cat does not give birth by the tenth week, discuss the overdue pregnancy with your vet. The veterinarian can decide if there are complications that require inducing labor.

A pregnant cat is not sick and should be allowed to move freely about her environment leading a normal life until labor ensues.

Do not give any medicine to a pregnant cat without specific instructions from your vet.

Feeding A Pregnant Cat

The expectant feline requires more food because she is providing nourishment for the unborn kittens. Give your pregnant female five to six ounces of meat each day. A small portion of boiled vegetables will help to prevent constipation. Offer ¼ teaspoon of steamed bone meal per day. This will provide the additional calcium and phosphorus required for healthy fetal bone growth and the production of milk.

Preparing For The Birth

As the onset of labor draws near your cat may become exceedingly affectionate. To aid nursing, it is a good idea to begin lubricating her teats with petroleum jelly or vitamin B oil a few days before the birth.

As your cat's belly grows larger she may have difficulty cleaning her anus. If this occurs, gently wash it with warm water.

Preparing The Nest

As the due date approaches you will want to have a place for the birth to occur already prepared. You do not want your cat to give birth in the closet, on the sofa, or in a drawer. Place a box or basket in a quiet, warm, and well-lit corner of your home. Put a soft blanket in the nest and cover it with a towel that can be changed daily. Locate a litter pan near the nest. Introduce your cat to this nesting area.

Do not let your cat give birth in the garage, cellar or backyard. It is dangerous to the health of both the mother and the kittens to let the birth occur in a cold, damp place. As her due date draws near keep your cat indoors. When your queen (a name for expecting cats) begins to produce milk, you know that labor is imminent.

At the moment of birth your cat will appear agitated and meow sweetly. When this occurs place her near the nesting place. Caress her head and womb gently as you speak in loving tones.

The Birth

It is very important for the birth to occur in a warm room. As the labor intensifies the cat's skin will become taut, the abdominal muscles will contract and the rate of respiration will increase. She will either assume a squatted or a stretched out position. During labor your cat's temperature will fall from the normal 100.5 F to approximately 98 F.

Within a few minutes the fetal sac will appear and a kitten will follow. If the kitten is to survive, the mother should remove it from the sac and clean it within ten minutes of the birth. If she does not, then you will need to rip the sac open gently. Wipe the kitten with a clean towel. Open its mouth to be sure it is free of fluid.

Mother cats free newborn kittens by biting the umbilical cord. If your cat is unable to accomplish this, tie the cord with clean thread and with sterilized scissors cut the cord above the thread.

A cat can give birth to as few as one and as many as five kittens. A prolific female can give birth to as many as twenty kittens a year, and within a year all of the females in any litter can give birth to as many as twenty kittens a year.

The placenta should be expelled after the birth of each kitten. If it is not expelled, use a clean cloth and pull gently and slowly on the cord. An unexpelled placenta can cause an infection. Once expelled it is normal for cats to eat the afterbirth.

If the birth of the kittens is premature, you may lose them. The survival rate for premature kittens is very low.

If a kitten is born dead or is the victim of a birth defect, the mother cat will sometimes destroy it by eating it. This is a natural law which cats have followed since antiquity.

Newborn Kittens

Avoid touching the newborn kittens. If the mother detects a strange or unfamiliar odor on the kitten, she may refuse to feed it. Kittens are born blind, deaf and toothless. Their eyes remain closed for eight to ten days. Newborn kittens are unable to walk, hence the mother cat will carry her kittens around for about two weeks or until they are strong enough to walk.

Nursing

Kittens should be nursed for a minimum of forty days, but not in excess of sixty days. Cat mothers are exceptionally loving and will encourage kittens to suckle a few minutes after birth. This early feeding is important to the kittens' survival.

The nutrient-rich cat mother's milk allows the kitten to double its birth weight within a week.

If a kitten is rejected or for some reason is unable to nurse, you will need to feed it artifically. Discuss the formula for the kitten with the vet. Newborn kittens should not be given cow's milk. You will need to give the kitten seven to eight feedings a day. A feeding for a newborn kitten approximates a teaspoonful of milk. However, discuss portions with your vet.

In the unfortunate circumstances of the mother's death the kitten must be kept sufficiently warm until it is old enough to regulate its own body heat. If possible try to find a female cat who is willing to care for the orphaned kittens. The licking and handling that mother cats give kittens is important to their physical and psychological well-being.

CHAPTER NINE

Everyday Living

There are elements of basic care that require your daily attention. Your cat will require food, water, clean litter, overt affection and ample exercise. There may be times when you will need to nurse your cat back to good health. Or times when you must administer emergency first aid. It is always important to keep stress in your cat's environment at a minimum. This chapter offers several ways to enhance and assure proper care of your pet.

Use Catnip Wisely
For the vast majority of cats the ecstasy of catnip is irresistible. Use a natural brand that is free of chemicals and additives. Catnip is a wonderful reward to a cat for good behavior, or just for fun. Use the catnip sparingly, however, giving your cat no more than two servings every seven days. Over exposure to catnip risks burning your cat out, or desensitizing him to a pleasant experience.

Keep Stress Out Of A Cat's Environment

Stress is a major part of a cat's life. The cat's physical body and psychological makeup are both very sensitive to its environment.

Disturbed by loud noise, abrupt movement, or unexpected intrusion, the supersensitive cat will react dramatically by snapping to attention out of a deep sleep, fleeing the room, or hiding out. Pungent odors, loud music, harsh voices, or rough activity all disturb your cat's psyche.

Cats experience many forms of stress. Many cats have mourned deeply the loss of a loved one. Cats miss vacationing owners and get depressed, sometimes losing their appetites. Cats placed in kennels exhibit nervous, tense behavior. A visit to the veterinarian, a ride in the cat carrier, or almost any change can cause the cat stress.

Cats prefer quiet, serene slow-to-change environments. Cats who live in noisy, chaotic environments will sleep a lot in far away corners trying to escape the stress-provoking atmosphere.

Unchecked stress in a cat's life can result in diminished health, disease, weight loss, withdrawal, tension, and nervous behavior.

Some of the more obvious forms of stress include: aggression by people or animals; keeping a cat confined in a small room or cage for indefinite periods of time; sexual frustration in the unneutered cat; life in the streets.

Many cats exhibit an acute sensitivity to the owner's moods and attitudes. Your nervous, anxious behavior will result in nervous behavior in your cat. Cats often sense an owner's state of happiness or unhappiness, fear, or pain.

Children who are untrained in dealing with cats can cause stress in felines. They will run from such children.

Never force a cat to play with a rough child. The cat can get hurt, the child scratched or bitten.

A Stressful Encounter:
Introducing A New Cat To The Old One

Accomplish the introduction of the new cat to the litter box with the door closed. Then open the door of the room, leaving it slightly ajar. Avoid obviously watching the behavior of the cats, but keep a watchful eye cast about. Allow your cat to discover the newcomer—that is, if the new cat has been issued a clean bill of health by the veterinarian before coming into the home. There may be some hissing and growling during the inspection. Do not get involved at this point. If an actual fight seems imminent, step in. Otherwise, let the cats establish a rapport. Do not be surprised if your cat's innate resistance to change makes him pretend to hurt the intruder, or ignore the new arrival for days.

Introducing A Mature Cat To A New Owner

When an old cat enters a new home, give it sufficient freedom to approach the owner after it has had time to acquaint itself with the surroundings and has received a few good meals. All this newness is a stressful change for the cat. Do not rush the cat and risk creating undesirable responses to your approach. Make sure the cat knows you are responsible for its food. Cats usually first display affection towards people who feed them.

You May Need To Care For A Sick Cat At Home

Unless hospitalization is required, it is much better for your cat to recover from an illness or injury at home. The shorter the cat's stay at the vet's the better. The cat experiences undue stress in the caged environment full of strange animals, people, sounds, and smells. The cat is also exposed to germs.

Depending upon the nature of your cat's illness or injury, you may be asked to perform a number of nursing duties. You may need to drain an abscess and flush it with an antibiotic solution. Or you may be required to give your cat oral medication. If you are called upon to perform any of these medical duties for your cat, carefully follow the veterinarian's instructions.

Restraining Your Cat

You may need to restrain your cat to administer the treatment. It helps when two people participate. But, if you are working alone, immobilize your cat by wrapping the cat's body in a towel. Place a large bath towel on your lap. Place the cat on its side on the towel and wrap the towel around the cat to restrain him. If you are working on a foot, wrap three legs. When two people participate one can hold the cat while the other executes the procedure. Never grasp your cat by the scruff of the neck to pick her up, but you can use this hold to medicate a squirming feline.

Remain calm throughout the restraining process as you speak to your cat in soothing, loving tones. Tell the cat what you are doing is good for him.

Giving Your Cat a Pill

Our cats have been remarkably free of sickness. We believe this is due to their high-quality diet. On one occasion the doctor prescribed an antibiotic to be given to all the cats at mealtime. We were instructed to cover the pill with a tiny amount of cat food. To assure the cat's ingestion of the antibiotic, we immediately gave the cats their regular plate of food.

We have heard of cat owners who have been instructed by the vet to crush the pills and mix them in with the food. However, there are medications that are best taken alone. Follow your vet's instructions when giving your cat medication. Do not mix it with food unless he has suggested that you do so. If you are uncertain, ask.

You can also coat the pill with butter or olive oil to make it slide easily down the cat's throat. If you are working alone, wrap the cat. If you have a partner, one person can hold the cat's abdomen to his chest with a gentle one-armed embrace. Exert just enough pressure to keep the cat in place. The person giving the pill should gently grasp the top of the cat's head behind the eyes. Drop the pill onto the center of the cat's tongue. Hold the cat's mouth shut until he swallows.

This is a stress-producing situation for your cat. Use gentle tones and provide plenty affection and stroking afterwards if your cat is disposed to accepting them.

When administering liquid medicine, give it slowly to avoid choking the cat. Apply the same method of restraint you need when giving a pill. Use an eye dropper or small syringe without the needle. Gently place the eye dropper into the right side of the mouth between the upper and lower teeth. The cat will respond by automatically opening her mouth a tiny bit. Administer the liquid slowly. Allow a short rest period whenever it seems the cat is getting too much. It is imperative that you are gentle, but you must be firm and display no sense of nervousness or trepidation. If you do so, your cat will become agitated.

Hairball medication, certain vitamins, and nutritional supplements come as paste. Some cats will take the paste directly from the tube. If your cat does not, place small amounts on his nose or the top of his paws. The cat will ingest the paste while cleaning himself. If the cat, with a flick of his paw, flips the paste away instead, gently spread the paste over his back teeth.

It Is Important To Provide Dental Care For Your Cat

All too often, informed owners, who maintain high-quality care of their pets, are completely unaware of the importance of oral hygiene for the cat. They are unaware that tartar and plaque buildup on the cat's teeth, if untreated, will eventually cause bad health.

Kittens are born without teeth, but develop baby teeth between four to five weeks, and cut permanent teeth by the age of six months.

Regular dental checkups are vital to your cat's good health. Annual cleanings are recommended. Diseases of the gums may cause serious illness, contributing to kidney, liver, and heart problems.

Discuss your cat's dental care needs with your vet.

You Can Clean Your Cat's Teeth

You can learn to clean your cat's teeth by using a soft toothbrush for cats, a soft cloth, or a piece of gauze wrapped around your finger.

Tooth decay and gum disease hurt your cat. Your cat's mouth might be giving her trouble if you notice frequent pawing at the mouth, loss of appetite, difficulty chewing, bad breath, or red, inflamed gums.

Emergency Care and First Aid

If your cat is wounded or exhibits life-threatening symptoms, call the vet at once. Explain the emergency and arrange to bring the cat in immediately. If this occurs on a weekend, or at night, many veterinarians have an emergency care number. Some animal hospitals operate twenty-four hour facilities.

The information that follows is provided only to aid you in giving any first aid treatments the veterinarian may ask you to carry out en route to the office.

Before approaching an injured cat make sure you have covered your hands and arms with lined leather, work, or gardening gloves to protect them from the frightened animal who may confuse you with the source of pain.

Approach slowly calling the cat by name and telling him your name. You should also cover the cat's feet to prevent it from scratching. Never muzzle the cat. If you find that you need to restrain your cat to help him, gently place a small blanket or large bath towel over the cat. Wrap his body. Do not cover the cat's head.

Check Your Cat's Vital Signs
A normal cat inhales and exhales at a rate of 25 to 30 breaths per minute. Notice the nature of your cat's breathing—is it slow and labored, or does the cat appear to be hyperventilating? If the cat is breathing irregularly, remove her collar and check the nose and mouth for obstructions.

Artificial Respiration
If your cat is not breathing, provide artificial respiration. Lay the cat on its side, and gently press on his rib cage with the palm of your hand, compressing it about once every two seconds. If the cat does not respond after several attempts, you may need to give mouth-to-mouth resuscitation. Open his mouth, pull his tongue forward and clear the throat of any obstruction, including blood and saliva. Then close the mouth, wrap your hand around his muzzle, cover his nose and mouth with your mouth, and blow gently once every two seconds. Between breaths remove your mouth so that the cat can exhale. Stop as soon as the cat starts to breathe on his own.

Shock

An injured cat can go into shock hours after an accident occurs. If you detect a rapid or feeble heartbeat, shallow breathing, pale or white gums and mouth, a cold body, confusion or unconsciousness, get your cat to the vet at once. Enroute, keep the cat warm by wrapping her in a blanket, towel, or shawl. Position the cat's head slightly lower than the rest of the body as you stroke and talk to her. Loosen the collar, pull the tongue forward and remove any vomit, blood or saliva.

Bleeding

You must stop profuse bleeding at once. Never try to administer a tourniquet. An improper tourniquet can completely cut off the flow of blood causing the death of tissue. Use a clean cloth to cover the wound and apply direct pressure. Wrap the cloth around the wound, applying a little pressure with each wrap. Tape or tie the cloth securely. If the area that is bleeding does not lend itself to wrapping, use a small cloth or gauze pads to apply pressure directly to the wound. Do not remove the pad once it becomes saturated, put another one on top. Secure the bandage firmly in place.

Clean a wound that is not bleeding excessively with peroxide or mild, soapy water. After the wound is clean, bandage it with an antiseptic dressing.

In all of the above mentioned scenarios, you must get immediate medical care for your cat. Sometimes, a wound may be worse than it appears, and will require treatment by a competent professional.

Force Feeding

To save your cat's life you may be required to force feed her when she loses her appetite. Never initiate this process on your own. Your veterinarian will recommend it when needed, and will provide the dietary components. Many veterinarians follow a diet that includes egg yolk, water, corn oil, and syrup.

A cat experiencing a devastating loss of appetite may respond to homemade chicken soup. Add brewer's yeast, and kelp to the broth and serve it to the cat. Include green and yellow vegetables in the soup. Some owners add a little cod liver oil to the broth. Others add chopped organ meat to cook along with the soup mixture.

Older Cats Have Special Needs

According to the *1990 Guinness Book of World Records* the oldest cat lived one day past his 36th birthday. The average cat will live between 13 and 18 years, depending upon breed and care. The slow physical decline of old age can first be noticed when a cat is between 10 and 12 years old. Cats who have been neutered tend to live longer. An older cat needs regular check-ups by the veterinarian more often than a younger one.

Take great care to make sure that the older cat gets all the nourishment it needs to ward off disease. Many older cats require food supplements because their digestion and food absorption becomes faulty.

Your Cat's Age Compared to Your Age	
Cat Age	Human Equivalent
1-month	5-6 months
5 months	8-9 years
1 year	18 years
5 years	40 years
10 years	60 years
15 years	74 years

The Sad Act Of Love

Euthanasia may be your only choice when the degradation of suffering outweighs the benefits of life. This humane gesture liberates the cat from unnecessary suffering.

The sudden loss of a beloved pet by mercy killing can invoke deep grief. Do not be ashamed of your grief, nor feel guilty if you know you've provided a good home for the cat. Some owners have sworn during the emotion-filled phase of grief that they will never own another cat. This is not the decision to make. Give yourself a few months to recover sufficiently from your grief and then give another cat a home.

Who Will Care For Your Cat When You Are Gone?

Although we never like to face the prospects of departing this life before a beloved pet, it is possible. Make arrangements with someone you trust to take over your cat if you should go away first. Solicit neighbors, friends or relatives who are avid animal lovers, to take your cats in if anything should happen to you. Provide for your cats in your will, leaving instructions for their care.

CHAPTER TEN

Cat Literacy:
What Every Cat Owner Should Know

Most behavioral problems are probably a result of misunderstanding the cat. Healthy, psychologically adjusted cats who are fed a high-quality diet, have plenty of fresh water, and a clean litter pan, are almost always on exemplary behavior. Cats are polite, respectful creatures, with extraordinary physical and mental balance.

Many actions that owners label "unacceptable behavior" occur in cats who are expressing the symptoms of impending, or fully bloomed ill health. Eating a nutrient deficient diet can cause poor behavior also.

"Finicky" Is Created By Owners.

Finicky cats are created by their owners. Cats become finicky from overeating. A cat fed a high-quality diet will have no need to overeat. It is unfortunate that so many owners overfeed cats, greatly hindering their ability to move about gracefully.

If your cat is overweight, before putting your cat on a

diet discuss it with the veterinarian. Never leave food out for more than half an hour around a cat who tends to overeat. If you have taken all the steps recommended in the chapter on nutrition to assure a highly nourishing diet for your cat, feel free to monitor his intake to prevent obesity. An obese cat can die of a virus that a healthy adult cat would be rid of with little treatment.

Use The Cautious Approach

Whenever you approach your cat to do something to him always begin the process with stroking and petting while speaking in soothing tones, as you tell the cat what you are about to do. Begin every activity that requires you to handle your cat this way. When you reach for a cat use just one hand, keeping the other in plain sight. Use this hand to stroke and calm the cat. This cautious approach does not overwhelm the cat.

Keep A Well Groomed Cat

Start brushing your cat from the time it is a kitten. Cats respond well, during a nap, to gentle brushing. Use a brush with natural bristles. If your cat has long hair, her coat must be combed and brushed daily. If the cat's hair becomes matted, consult a groomer with previous experience in removing mats. When selecting a groomer for your long-haired cat, avoid those who specialize in dogs. The needs of dogs and cats are quite different. Select a groomer with demonstrated experience in handling cats, one who displays great affection and love for the feline.

Many veterinarians recommend a wire brush with fine metal teeth and two types of combs: a coarse comb with ten to fourteen teeth per inch and a fine metal comb with twenty rigid teeth per inch.

Cats have very delicate skin, so be very gentle. You can

decrease the likelihood of large hair balls substantially by combing and brushing your cat's coat frequently. When you are grooming your cat be sure to comb and brush the sides of the cat's head, the back of the neck, "underarms", and stomach. Never brush down the cat's delicate spine. Always brush away from the cat's spine toward the sides.

Groom short hair cats with a fine tooth comb. Groom longhair cats, such as persians and angoras, with a coarse comb.

If you are not inclined to have your cat groomed regularly by a professional, but would like the advice of one, Anitra Frazier's *The Natural Cat: A Wholistic Guide For Finicky Owners* contains an excellent step-by-step description of grooming and instructions for removing mats. Avoid shaving mats because it is painful and may scratch or cut the sensitive feline skin. Matted hair forms as a result of insufficient grooming.

Your Cat's Ears And Eyes

During the grooming session examine your cats ears. Clean wax build-up gently with a cotton swab lighly moistened in Vitamin E oil.

A healthy cat's ear canal contains a small amount of honey colored ear wax. If, however, you detect a bad odor your cat may be infested with ear mites.

Mucous build-up in your cat's eyes is a sign of irritation. Moisten a cotton ball with water, lightly pass it over from the inner side to the outside of the face.

Protect The Cat's Skin

During the grooming session examine your cat thoroughly. A glossy coat and clear skin are primary signs of a healthy cat. Healthy undamaged skin is a barrier to disease.

Many house cats who spend the winter months indoors experience dry skin. Cat skin needs plenty of Vitamins A, D, and E and certain fatty acids. If you notice dry flaky skin, notify your vet. Add a half teaspoon of cod liver oil to the daily diet of a cat with dry skin. It is a good idea to supplement the diet of a cat with healthy skin by serving cod liver oil several times a week.

Never Cut a Cat's Whiskers

The whiskers are the most sensitive component of the cat's extraordinary anatomical sensory system. The whiskers sense the slightest touch. The whiskers allow the cat to "see" in the dark by perceiving the presence and nature of an object. The sensitive whiskers sense air currents so that your cat feels moving objects approaching even when his back is turned. A loss of whiskers greatly obstructs the cat's ability to move about.

The Cat's Powerful Sense Of Smell

Cats use their sense of small to interpret, define, and understand their environment. No odor escapes the cat. The cat can detect aromas that humans cannot. A cat's food is not appreciated by its taste, but by its smell. Incidentally it is the smell of catnip that attracts the cat.

A cat knows the scent of beloved friends. Certain viruses can cause the cat to lose his sense of smell resulting in a loss of appetite.

Bathing

Bathing cats is generally not recommended, but there may be instances where your cat becomes soiled and will need a bath. Always comb and brush the cat's hair before bathing. Use a protein rich, mild or baby, no-tear shampoo.

The kitchen sink or a small tub are ideal places for bathing your cat.

A Wet Cat Is Susceptible To Infection

Remove all excess water with a large bath towel. Use a blow dryer on a low setting to complete the drying. Towel and brush as you blow dry. Give the bath in a warn environment because a chilled cat is susceptible to infection. Do not allow the cat to go into a drafty area for several hours following the bath.

Dogs And Cats

When roaming the wilderness freely, dogs and cats clashed violently. Their contact with human beings has meant centuries of living in harmony. In these modern times fighting dogs and cats are the exception rather than the rule. In numerous households dogs and cats enjoy a peaceful, harmonious existence.

Traveling And Your Cat

There will be times when you must stay away from your cat overnight, entrusting your beloved pet's well-being to others. Plan ahead. Line up a friend of the cat to care for her in your home, or in their home, if you are suddenly called away on an emergency.

When you are planning a trip, enlist a dependable service, friend or relative who is willing to watch your cat during your trips. Placing the sensitive cat in a kennel for an extended period should be assiduously avoided. However, the kennel is better than a cat left untended or abandoned. You'd be surprised at the number of cats that are abandoned to the streets when their owners go on vacation.

The ideal cat sitter will be familiar to the cat, will sleep over, and will carefully follow your instructions. If you are unable to get someone to sleep over, then ask the person to spend some time stroking and consoling the cat during the visits for feeding. If you cannot get someone to come into your home find a cat lover who exemplifies your high standards and board the cat in this household. If the hour of your departure is very near and you have not found a suitable plan for your cat, you will have to board your feline in a kennel. Since your cat will be caged for the better part of the time that you are away, the standards of cleanliness should be very high. Sick animals should be kept away from healthy ones. Cats should be separated from dogs. The quality of the diet should be high and well supplemented to protect the cat from the inevitable streess. The keepers should have a deep respect and love for cats.

Many cats learn to travel in cars and other motor vehicles. It is a good idea not to feed the cat for twelve hours before the trip or give water within four hours of the trip. Cats can become accustomed to travel. Nevertheless, it can be an agitating experience for the cat's delicate system. In this agitated state, your feline may become startled and attempt to flee. To avoid the horror of having your cat become a traffic fatality, during a car trip, place the cat in a carrier.

Planes, trains, and bus lines all have regulations governing the travel of pets. Avoid having your cat travel in the baggage area of a bus, plane or train. Many airlines permit pets to travel on board with the owner. When travelling with your cat, provide a calm environment filled with quiet love and affection to assist it through the ordeal of traveling.

Beware of Giving Your Cat Drugs

Cats are very sensitive to drugs of all kinds (legal and illegal). Do not even give your cat aspirin. Give your cat medication prescribed by the vet only.

Cats, Babies, And Kids

The arrival of a new baby is an exciting time for families. However, you must prepare your cat. Cats will react with anxiety to dramatic alterations of their environment. This natural reaction is incorrectly labeled as "jealousy." Before the baby is brought home, allow the cat to examine the nursery so that it can become familiar with the baby's furniture and accessories. If possible, bring something home from the hospital with the baby's scent on it. Do not ignore your pet when you bring the new baby home. To do so can cause behavioral problems.

Do not leave the infant alone with the cat, but do not discipline the cat for coming near the baby. Reward the cat when it demonstrates acceptable behavior around the infant.

Insure a happy situation by keeping your cat's nails clipped. Supervise the cat's visits with the infant; be pleasant with your cat when he is with the baby.

A devoted and loving cat as a pet can greatly boost a child's self-esteem. Your child learns responsibility as it fulfills the chores of caring for the cat. However, never put the complete responsibility for the care of the pet on the child. Teach your children: not to pull the cat's tail or ears; not to hold on to the cat if he wants to go; not to disturb a sleeping or eating cat; not to disturb the cat in his litter box; to never play in the litter; and to let the cat approach them.

CHAPTER ELEVEN

Intelligence, Behavior, Personality
And Breeds

Cats are intelligent, but make reluctant trainees. There is little that is servile in the cat's nature. For no other reward than to please their masters, dogs will quickly learn to fetch, hunt, play games, and more. Cats learn only what brings clear benefit to them.

When it is to the cat's advantage, a cat can be trained to open a door, offer a paw, or to fetch. Young cats are far more likely to respond to such training than adult cats with well-established patterns of behavior.

Cats often display their intelligence by learning something on their own such as knocking on a window to get in, and grabbing the door knob to get out.

You can, however, train your cat to obey if you provide a climate of affection and the action you seek ends with something the cat desires.

The Famous Meow And The Fabulous Purr
The two cat sounds are the meow and the purr. Cats

are said to emit as many as fifty different tone variations in meow. Like Chinese, mew is a tonal language. Alert owners can recognize joy, pain, delight, fear, anxiety, hunger, or sickness in the cat's meow. Siamese are well known for their ability to express themselves vocally. The cat's purr expresses joy, well being, and affection. A loudly purring cat is a happy cat.

Breeds

Breeds generally refer to pedigreed cats who can trace a distinctive geneaology. There are more than forty cat breeds. Although the basic framework of "the cat personality" applies to all breeds of cats, each has a special characteristic.

Adult persian/longhair cats are placid, difficult to care for, and like Angoras and Balinese they must be combed every day. The long haired breeds prefer cool spaces. Oriental breeds, the Siamese in particular, are high strung. Siamese cats require much affection and prefer warm spaces. The American shorthair loves to play with children. The chatreux is a tenacious hunter of mice, while British and European shorthairs are very sweet.

The Housecat

These cats once regarded as alley cats or mongrels are the offsprings of random breeding. Although their outward appearance resembles the pedigree breeds, the personality traits in these cats may vary. Like their pedigreed cousins, random breed cats come in a variety of colors, including: white, black, gray, blue-gray, red, cream, silver, chinchilla.

The Character Of A Good Cat

The ideal cat is cordial with people, loves to be indoors, does not scratch outside the scratching area, and is scrupulously clean. Most mixed breed cats possess these good qualities with intelligence sometimes surpassing the purebreds.

Should You Ever Punish A Cat?

Rarely should you punish a cat. Never use threatening objects like brooms against a cat. Never use screaming, noisy reprimands. A firm no and a squirt of water, in the face, from a water pistol at the same time the cat performs that unwanted act can, over time, train a cat to act differently.

Your Hands Are Instruments Of Love

Never strike your cat with your hands. You want your cat to see your hands as instruments of love.

Respect The Cat's Independence

The cat's independent nature is seen in the feline ability to spend considerable periods of time alone quite contentedly.

Let Your Cat Approach You

If you are gentle, kind and calm with her, your cat will freely offer you affection, rubbing, snuggling, licking and purring. Cats, by nature, tend to be gentle toward people. An aggressive cat is usually the product of an aggressive owner.

Inappropriate Elimination

The fastidious cat will not use a filthy litter box. Longhair cats have an even greater concern as they may get waste on the long hairs (called bloomers) of their thighs. Cats will also shun a litter box when the type of litter has been changed abruptly.

Cats may frequently return to an area outside of the litter box where the odor of previous elimination is present. Deodorize the area to discourage a repeat performance. There are preparations available from your veterinarian or a pet store. If your cat consistently eliminates in the same spot, place the litter box over that spot. After the cat has begun to use the litter box again, gradually move it back to the preferred place.

Several illnesses of the urinary tract often will not allow the cat enough time to get to the litter box. If your cat is demonstrating unusual patterns of elimination, he may be ill. Take the cat to the vet for a thorough checkup. Take a stool sample along with you. A cat undergoing emotional stress—the prolonged absence of the owner—may come down with cystitis which causes frequent urination.

Stress in the environment may alter your cat's elimination habits. Such emotional trauma include moving to a new home; visitors who upset the cat; the loss of a beloved owner; a new cat is introduced; a food change is made or any significant change in environment or routine. Fighting and loud arguments between household members can cause emotional upset to a sensitive cat.

Ignore A Cat's Aggressive Behavior

It is unheard of for a cat to attack a human being. Just ignore the aggressive cat. If it is aggressive toward another animal, separate the antagonists.

Be consistent. If you see the cat approaching a forbidden spot stand in front of the cat between him and the table or chair and calmly, firmly say no.

If your cat jumps onto a table or couch before you can stop him or you walk into the room and find the cat perched on the off limits territory, push the cat off as you firmly say no.

The independent, intelligent, lovable feline can be trained to live quite respectfully in your home.

Cats are remarkable companions. The energy you invest in caring for your feline friend will pay off in years of love and devotion from your cat.

Elza Dinwiddie-Boyd is a teacher and writer based in New York. She has published several non-fiction books and is the mother of three cats.

INDEX